LOVE

Proverbs of the Heart

LOVE
Proverbs of the Heart

Wolfgang Mieder

Silhouettes by Kim S. Holtan

The New England Press
Shelburne, Vermont

Library of Congress Catalog Card Number: 89-63662
ISBN 0-933050-63-1

For additional copies of this book or for
a catalog of our other titles, please write:

The New England Press
P.O. Box 575
Shelburne, VT 05482

Contents

Introduction

The great poets of the world have found innumerable ways to express the unique feeling of love. Early classical literature, medieval love lyrics, and the epic poem of *Tristan and Isolde* still move the hearts of modern readers. William Shakespeare's plays and especially his sonnets abound with unforgettable expressions of love, and Elizabeth Barrett Browning's love poetry continues to touch people sensitive to the wonders of love. Anthologists have put together entire books of poems or quotations dealing with the many aspects of love. These poetic reflections upon love have allowed readers throughout the centuries to experience vicariously the joys and sorrows of this deep human emotion. Those in love have been able to identify with these poetic and seemingly universal statements.

But there exists another tradition of valuable insights into love that has been handed down orally among people of all nations and ethnic backgrounds. Anonymous "poets" from among the folk have crystallized their thoughts on love into short but poetic statements. What started out at any given time in the past as an acute observation on the ways of love by a particular individual was picked up by members of that society and finally gained common currency in the form of a generally known proverb. Such proverbs are short, well-known sentences of the folk that contain wisdom, truth, morals, and traditional views in a metaphorical, fixed, and memorizable form handed down from generation to generation. By the time such a concise piece of wisdom concerning everyday occurrences became proverbial through repetitive use, its individual author was usually long forgotten and the proverb had come to be used as an anonymous expression of a basic truth whenever it fit strategically into a certain situation. A couple of English proverbs even state that "All the good sense of the world runs in proverbs" and "Proverbs are the children of experience." There is no doubt that proverbs contain a good dose of common sense, experience, wisdom, and above all truth about every imaginable situation of life.

Since love is one of the fundamental human emotions, it is not surprising that there are hundreds of proverbs that comment on it in the languages of the world. They are differentiated from other literary statements due to their traditionality and such poetic or stylistic features as alliteration, rhyme, parallelism, ellipsis, repetition, personification, hyperbole, paradox, and the like. Short proverb texts such as "Love makes labor light," "Where hearts are true, few words will do," "Good luck in cards, bad luck in marriage," "Cold hands, warm heart," "Love makes time pass away, and time makes love pass away," "Love laughs at locksmiths," "The lover who suffers not anguish knows not the worth of pleasure," and "Short love brings a long sigh"—all are simple poetic expressions. What is more, they really are known and used repeatedly by people in all walks of life. While they might not be as romantic and original in language and tone as literary reflections on love, proverbs certainly contain the folk's thoughts on love in short individual observations that present a realistic view of love. It is exactly the realism and honesty of proverbs on love that make these gems of wisdom such crucial communicative devices.

It should surprise no one that proverbs on love contradict each other, just as proverbs in general do. Such contradictory pairs of proverbs as "Repentance comes too late" and

"Never too late to mend" or "Marry in haste and repent at leisure" and "Happy the wooing that's not long a-doing" reflect differences in attitude. People choose one of these texts as a strategy to react to a particular situation. The most well-known English contradictory-proverb pair is without doubt "Absence makes the heart grow fonder" and "Out of sight, out of mind." Only the specific situation and the attitude of the person reacting to it decide which of the two texts fits. When it comes to proverb usage, one can truly argue that "If the proverb fits, use it." What such contradictory proverb-pairs make absolutely clear is that proverbs are not universal truths but rather expressions of wisdom limited to particular contexts and intentions.

Proverbs such as "One hand washes the other" and "Man does not live by bread alone" (Matt.4:4) go back to classical times or the wisdom literature of the Talmud and the Bible. These old proverbs were translated into many languages and they survive in identical forms to the present day. Love proverbs such as "Love is blind," "Love and a cough cannot be hid," and even "Out of sight, out of mind" are all of Latin origin and are known in numerous modern languages. These international proverbs have to a certain degree become overused clichés. Clearly of greater interest are proverbs that have no direct parallels in other cultures, such as

"Love lives in palaces as well as in thatched cottages" (Japanese), "The fire of lust is more fierce than a smoking fire" (Indian—Tamil), "A pair of women's breasts has more pulling power than a pair of oxen" (Mexican), "Frequent kisses end in a baby" (Hungarian), and "Love does not choose the blade of grass on which it falls" (African—Zulu). Here the reader finds metaphors of love that are at least in part dependent on a particular culture.

In order to show international similarities and national differences in the world's proverbs on love, this book contains over five hundred texts from literally dozens of proverb collections. Among them are many of ancient origin that have become current in English and other languages. The Latin proverb "*Amor caecus*" exists, for example, in direct English translation as "Love is blind," in French as "*L'amour est aveugle*," in German as "*Die Liebe ist blind*," in Italian as "*L'amore è cieco*," in Spanish as "*El amor es ciego*," in Russian as "*Liubov' slepa*," and so on. Such international proverbs are listed in this collection as belonging to the English language without referring to the dozens of languages into which they have also been translated. For this reason there are no specific references to ancient Greek, Latin, or biblical proverbs.

It is also possible, for example, to find a proverb in this collection with a French-language designation, although it exists in Italian or perhaps another Romance language as well. In such cases, it is extremely difficult to ascertain in which language and culture the proverb did in fact originate. This is particularly true when two languages are linguistically and geographically very close, such as Spanish and Portuguese, German and Dutch, Danish and Swedish, and so on. To establish the definite linguistic origin of each proverb in this collection would have meant over five hundred searches. This clearly could not have been done and is not the purpose of this book. Each proverb therefore receives only one linguistic reference—to the language in which it is especially well known today.

While many proverbs in this collection differ considerably in their metaphors about such matters as passion, courtship, marriage, heartaches, and so on, they often still express the same idea. Thus, the Germans say that "Where there's no jealousy, there's no love," the Italians quote "Hot love is seldom without jealousy," and the Scots claim that "Love is never without jealousy." The English feel that "The greatest hate springs from the greatest love," while the Rumanians comment on the same idea with the proverb, "Love beyond measure afterward brings hatred." Such proverbs show that people from different cultures have created similar proverbs for the same idea, observation, or feeling. The experiences of love are quite universal, and one should expect that equivalent proverbs would have been formulated independently. In other words, similar proverbs do not necessarily have a common classical origin. For such basic emotions as love, passion, or hate, equivalent proverbs may well be indigenous to various national languages.

Yet the real charm of this collection of love proverbs from around the world lies in the colorful metaphoric language of the texts. Such proverbs as "Love is meat and drink, and a blanket to boot" (American), "The quarrels of married couples and the west wind stop at evening" (Japanese), "Love is like dew that falls on both nettles and lilies" (Swedish), "There is no such fiery love that would not be cooled down by marriage" (Russian), "He who marries for love has good nights and bad days" (French), "When husband and wife agree with each other, they can dry up the ocean with buckets" (Vietnamese), and others indicate the folk's wisdom regarding love relationships. These texts are neither saccharine nor sentimental but rather realistic, satirical, ironic, and even humorous. Love in these proverbs is not presented as a romantic ideal but instead as a fact of life.

Together these proverbs reflect the world-view of various peoples on the theme of love in thirteen small chapters. While the individual texts show the joys and sorrows, the ups and downs, and the pros and cons of all that love entails, collectively they add up to the proverbial wisdom that "It's love that makes the world go 'round." They express the wishes, dreams, and also the frustrations that people in love have experienced over the centuries and that future lovers will also encounter. In that regard, this little book of folk wisdom is indeed a treasure-trove of proverbs on the universal theme of love.

LOVE'S WAYS

Love laughs at locksmiths.
(*English*)

With a sweetheart you can have
paradise in a hut.
(*Russian*)

Love teaches asses to dance.
(*French*)

True love suffers no concealment.
(*Spanish*)

Love has made heroes of many and
fools of many more.
(*Swedish*)

Love grows with obstacles.
(*German*)

Love demands faith, and faith firmness.
(*Italian*)

In love there are no distinctions
between high and low.
(*Japanese*)

No fate is worse than a life
without a love.
(*Mexican*)

Love needs no teaching.
(*English*)

Love makes labor light.
(*Dutch*)

True love is sweet until the end.
(*Philippine*)

Love and fear cannot be hidden.
(*Russian*)

Love will find a way.
(*English*)

Love me, love my dog.
(*English*)

Love is like dew that falls on both
nettles and lilies.
(*Swedish*)

Love, a cough, and smoke will
not remain secret.
(*French*)

A tongue is not necessary
to declare love.
(*Welsh*)

Love cannot be compelled.
(*English*)

Where love reigns, the impossible
may be attained.
(*Indian—Tamil*)

Love is master of all arts.
(*Italian*)

The only present love demands is love.
(*English*)

Love needs no laws.
(*Slovakian*)

Love keeps the cold out better
than a cloak.
(*English*)

An old love is lasting.
(*Russian*)

Love makes men orators.
(*English*)

A secret love is always a true love.
(*Slovakian*)

Love knows hidden paths.
(*German*)

Love makes a wit of the fool.
(*English*)

To those we love best, we say the least.
(*Philippine*)

Love can make any place agreeable.
(*Egyptian*)

Love does not depend on our will.
(*French*)

Love warms more than
a thousand fires.
(*English*)

Who loves not wine, women, and song
remains a fool his whole life long.
(*German*)

Love will creep where it cannot go.
(*English*)

Love is love's reward.
(*English*)

True love shows itself in time of need.
(*Scottish*)

Love drives out fear.
(*Czech*)

Love conquers all.
(*English*)

Love fears no danger.
(*German*)

Where love is, there's no lack.
(*English*)

One always returns to one's
first love.
(*French*)

Love is like fog—there is no
mountain on which it does not rest.
(*Hawaiian*)

Sound love is not soon forgotten.
(*English*)

Old love does not rust.
(*German*)

Love rules its kingdom
without a sword.
(*English*)

Love defies law.
(*Indian—Bihar*)

Love to live and live to love.
(*English*)

Love lives in palaces as well as
in thatched cottages.
(*Japanese*)

Love is stronger than death.
(*French*)

Old love burns strong.
(*English*)

Love knows not labor.
(*Italian*)

It's love that makes the
world go 'round.
(*English*)

HEARTBEATS

A letter from the heart can be
read on the face.
(*African—Swahili*)

The heart does not lie.
(*Dutch*)

You can look in the eye, but not
in the heart.
(*Yiddish*)

A sweet tongue hides a bad heart.
(*Jamaican*)

Cold hands, warm heart.
(*German*)

When we love, it is the heart
that judges.
(*French*)

Satisfaction of the heart is
better than wealth.
(*Turkish*)

If the eyes don't see, the heart
won't break.
(*Spanish*)

A broken hand works, but not
a broken heart.
(*Iranian*)

The joy of the heart makes
the face merry.
(*English*)

When the heart is in love, beauty
is of no account.
(*Pashto*)

Words that come from the heart
enter the heart.
(*Hebrew*)

If hope were not, the heart
would break.
(*English*)

A loving heart is more precious
than gold.
(*Philippine*)

What the eyes do not see, the heart
does not desire.
(*Russian*)

Where hearts are true, few
words will do.
(*English*)

That which is far from the eye
is far from the heart.
(*Turkish*)

A heart is a lock, but a lock can
be opened with a duplicated key.
(*Yiddish*)

Fire in the heart sends smoke
into the head.
(*German*)

Were it not for hope, the heart
would break.
(*Scottish*)

The mouth is the interpreter
of the heart.
(*Estonian*)

Mouth and heart are far apart.
(*German*)

Heart finds a way to heart.
(*Iranian*)

A woman's heart is as changeable
as the eyes of a cat.
(*Japanese*)

Absence makes the heart grow fonder.
(*English*)

A woman's heart sees more than
ten men's eyes.
(*Swedish*)

One heart feels another's affections.
(*Yiddish*)

Let your heart go, and it will lead
you into slavery.
(*Russian*)

Hearts may agree though heads differ.
(*English*)

The ailment of the heart is
known to one only.
(*African—Zulu*)

Hope deferred makes the heart sick.
(*English*)

Out of sight, out of heart.
(*Lebanese*)

Sweet-melon lips, bitter-melon heart.
(*Chinese*)

Two things do prolong your life:
a quiet heart and a loving wife.
(*English*)

The tongue is the pen of the heart.
(*Yiddish*)

What the eyes see, the heart believes.
(*German*)

A maiden's heart is a dark forest.
(*Russian*)

Faint heart never won fair lady.
(*English*)

When the sight leaves the eye,
love leaves the heart.
(*Irish*)

Every heart has its secrets.
(*Yiddish*)

PASSION

The fire of lust is more fierce
than a smoking fire.
(*Indian—Tamil*)

A man in passion rides a horse that
runs away with him.
(*English*)

Lust leads to love.
(*Hebrew*)

Maidens say no and do it all the same.
(*German*)

When passionately in love,
one becomes stupid.
(*Japanese*)

A flood can be controlled,
but lust never.
(*Philippine*)

In sleep man doesn't sin, but
his dreams do.
(*Yiddish*)

Hot passion cools easily.
(*Japanese*)

It is not reason that governs love.
(*French*)

Love or fire in your trousers is
not easy to conceal.
(*Swedish*)

There is no such fiery love that
would not be cooled down by marriage.
(*Russian*)

A maid that gives, yields.
(*English*)

Short pleasure often brings
long repentance.
(*Danish*)

Love's a malady without a cure.
(*English*)

In love and war, no time
should be lost.
(*English*)

Don't be so much in love that you
can't tell when the rain is coming.
(*Malagasy*)

A beautiful girl's cheeks are
the foes of her chastity.
(*Greek*)

A woman's petticoat is
the devil's binder.
(*Rumanian*)

Love is a talkative passion.
(*English*)

Too much love causes heartbreak.
(*Philippine*)

When passion enters at the foregate,
wisdom goes out at the postern.
(*English*)

Pleasures steal away the mind.
(*Dutch*)

Forbidden fruit is sweet.
(*English*)

The extreme form of passionate love
is secret love.
(*Japanese*)

Lust causes a man to break into
a house and rob.
(*Indian—Kashmiri*)

Love is without reason.
(*English*)

Shameless craving must have
a shameless nay.
(*English*)

Girls are wont to say no with their
lips, but with their eyes they say yes.
(*Mexican*)

Lust is the oldest lion of them all.
(*Italian*)

Short pleasure, long lament.
(*English*)

Idleness breeds lust.
(*Chinese*)

When the heart is full of lust,
the mouth is full of lies.
(*Scottish*)

Young lovers wish,
and married men regret.
(*Indian—Hindustani*)

They love too much that die for love.
(*English*)

Become not intoxicated, and you
will not sin.
(*Hebrew*)

Hot love is soon cold.
(*English*)

For lovesickness there is no medicine.
(*Japanese*)

Talking of love is making it.
(*English*)

If not for pretty girls, temptation
would be unheeded.
(*Yiddish*)

A pair of women's breasts has more
pulling power than a pair of oxen.
(*Mexican*)

There is no medicine for
sexual passion.
(*Japanese*)

Hasty love is soon hot and soon cold.
(*English*)

Every maid is undone.
(*English*)

Lust longs only for things forbidden.
(*Hebrew*)

He that has love in his breast has
spurs in his sides.
(*English*)

Love often gets the better of reason.
(*French*)

COURTSHIP

Even the wisest girl will yield to
the boy who perseveres in his wooing.
(*Vietnamese*)

If the girls won't run after the
men, the men will run after them.
(*American*)

Courting and baking don't
always succeed.
(*German*)

It's the last suitor that wins the maid.
(*Irish*)

As is the lover, so is the beloved.
(*Italian*)

When the groom is desired,
the bride doesn't need words.
(*Yiddish*)

The oaths of one who loves a woman
are not to be believed.
(*Spanish*)

He that would the daughter win must
with the mother first begin.
(*English*)

Lovers know well what they want but
not what they will get.
(*Dutch*)

He who likes to court doesn't like
to get married.
(*Polish*)

A man has choice to begin love,
but not to end it.
(*English*)

Better to break off an engagement
than a marriage.
(*Yiddish*)

A maiden with many wooers often
chooses the worst.
(*Scottish*)

33

When you go to dance, take heed
whom you take by the hand.
(*Danish*)

Happy is the wooing that is not
long a-doing.
(*English*)

Too much courting leads to ruin.
(*German*)

He who loves many won't marry any.
(*Philippine*)

He who flatters the mother will
hug the daughter.
(*Estonian*)

She is a woman and therefore
may be wooed; she is a woman and
therefore may be won.
(*English*)

Courting is better than burning.
(*Danish*)

Sweet talk makes the girls melt.
(*Yiddish*)

A short courtship is the best courtship.
(*Manx*)

Where love is in the case,
the doctor is an ass.
(*English*)

Let him not be a lover who
has not courage.
(*Italian*)

Observe the mother and take
the daughter.
(*Turkish*)

With nets you catch birds,
and with presents girls.
(*Yiddish*)

Men dream in courtship but
in wedlock wake.
(*English*)

He who has the luck brings
home the bride.
(*German*)

A man may woo where he will, but
wed where his wife is.
(*Scottish*)

A man chases a woman until
she catches him.
(*American*)

GETTING MARRIED

Marrying is easy,
but housekeeping is hard.
(*German*)

Always say no, and you will
never be married.
(*French*)

To get married is to tie a knot
with the tongue that you can't undo
with your teeth.
(*English*)

See the mother, and then
marry the daughter.
(*Rumanian*)

He who marries ill is long in
becoming widowed.
(*Spanish*)

One daughter helps to marry the other.
(*Italian*)

When an old man marries a young
wife, he becomes young and she old.
(*Yiddish*)

Happy is she who marries the son
of a dead mother.
(*Scottish*)

A maiden marries to please her
parents, a widow to please herself.
(*Chinese*)

Do not marry your lover, and never
take back the man you have divorced.
(*Lebanese*)

He who marries a beauty
marries trouble.
(*African—Yoruba*)

When a divorced man marries
a divorced woman, there are four
opinions in the marriage bed.
(*Hebrew*)

Before you marry, make sure of
a house wherein to tarry.
(*English*)

A man is often too young to marry,
but a man is never too old to love.
(*Finnish*)

Married today, marred tomorrow.
(*French*)

He that marries late marries ill.
(*English*)

Marry and grow tame.
(*Spanish*)

He who marries does well, but who
remains single does better.
(*German*)

Look at the mother before you take
her daughter in marriage.
(*Indian—Tamil*)

He who marries a young woman gets
welfare and a treasure.
(*Moroccan*)

It's good to marry late or never.
(*English*)

It is better to marry a quiet fool
than a witty scold.
(*English*)

Marry above your match, and you
get a master.
(*Scottish*)

When one buys a buffalo one looks
at his hoofs; when one marries a
woman one looks into her ancestry.
(*Vietnamese*)

Everyone sings as he has the gift,
and marries as he has the luck.
(*Portuguese*)

A quarrelsome girl will not be married.
(*African—Ovambo*)

He who marries might be sorry;
he who does not will be sorry.
(*Czech*)

To marry once is a duty, twice a
folly, thrice is madness.
(*Dutch*)

He that marries a maiden, marries
a pokeful of pleasure.
(*Scottish*)

Marry in haste, repent at leisure.
(*English*)

Before you marry reflect, for it is
a knot you cannot untie.
(*Portuguese*)

He who marries early
makes no mistake.
(*Turkish*)

If one will not, another will;
so are all maidens married.
(*Scottish*)

Married in a hurry and stuck for good!
(*Yiddish*)

Always in love, never married.
(*French*)

He has great need of a wife that
marries mama's darling.
(*English*)

Daughters are easy to rear,
but hard to marry.
(*German*)

Marry first, and love will follow.
(*English*)

Before you marry, consider
what you do.
(*Portuguese*)

Inquire about the mother before
you marry a girl.
(*Lebanese*)

Marrying and dying are two things
for which one is never late.
(*Yiddish*)

Honest men do marry, but
wise men not.
(*English*)

Marry your son when you will,
your daughter when you can.
(*Danish*)

He who marries for love has good
nights and bad days.
(*French*)

MARRIAGE

The best part of marriage is from
the day of engagement to the wedding.
(*Maltese*)

Marriage leaps up upon the saddle,
and repentance upon the crupper.
(*English*)

Love is a flower that turns into
fruit at marriage.
(*Finnish*)

Marriage is a lottery in which men
stake their liberty and women
their happiness.
(*French*)

Don't praise marriage on the third
day, but after the third year.
(*Russian*)

A woman does not perish in marriage.
(*African—Jabo*)

Hasty marriage seldom proves well.
(*English*)

Marriage and cooking call
for forethought.
(*Greek*)

The woman cries before the wedding
and the man after.
(*Polish*)

Marriages are made in heaven.
(*English*)

After the wedding, it's too late
to have regrets.
(*Yiddish*)

A compulsory marriage
does not endure.
(*Japanese*)

It will not always be honeymoon.
(*English*)

Marriage is not a race; you can
always get there in time.
(*Russian*)

Early marriage, long love.
(*German*)

Marriage is a lottery.
(*English*)

In marriage, cheat who can.
(*French*)

Marriage with the first wife is
made in heaven, with the second
it's arranged by people.
(*Yiddish*)

Wedlock is a lane where there
is no turning.
(*English*)

Love is a fair garden,
and marriage a field of nettles.
(*Finnish*)

Even a good marriage is a time of trial.
(*Russian*)

Marriage and hanging go by destiny.
(*English*)

Good luck in cards, bad
luck in marriage.
(*English*)

Marriages are not as they are made,
but as they turn out.
(*Italian*)

Where there's marriage without love,
there will be love without marriage.
(*English*)

A marriage between a young man and
an old woman is made by the devil.
(*Philippine*)

The marriage ceremony takes only an
hour, but its troubles last a lifetime.
(*Yiddish*)

A wedding lasts a day or two,
but the misery forever.
(*Czech*)

Marriage halves our griefs, doubles
our joys, and quadruples our expenses.
(*English*)

If marriages be made in heaven,
some had few friends there.
(*Scottish*)

45

Marriage is no joke; it is not like
rice, which can be spat out if
it is too hot.
(*Philippine*)

One wedding begets another.
(*English*)

Marriage is heaven and hell.
(*German*)

Love has wings on its shoulders;
matrimony has crutches under its arms.
(*Russian*)

Motions are not marriages.
(*English*)

Marriage without good faith is like
a teapot without a tray.
(*Moroccan*)

Age and wedlock tame man and beast.
(*English*)

Marriage is not like a patch that
you can take off whenever you like.
(*Maltese*)

Marriage is the tomb of love.
(*Russian*)

He has a great fancy to marriage
that goes to the devil for a wife.
(*English*)

Marriage is not a mere trial;
it is forever.
(*Philippine*)

One marriage is never celebrated
but another grows out of it.
(*German*)

An ill marriage is a spring
of ill fortune.
(*English*)

Marriage is an evil—but a
necessary evil.
(*Greek*)

Wedlock is a padlock.
(*English*)

The saloonkeeper loves the drunkard,
but he wouldn't give him his
daughter in marriage.
(*Yiddish*)

More belongs to marriage than four
bare legs in a bed.
(*English*)

47

HUSBAND AND WIFE

A deaf husband and a blind wife are
always a happy couple.
(*French*)

A good wife and health are a
man's best wealth.
(*English*)

When husband and wife agree with
each other, they can dry up the
ocean with buckets.
(*Vietnamese*)

Without a husband you are naked;
without a companion you are in need.
(*African—Ovambo*)

The more a husband loves his wife,
the more he increases her whims.
(*Chinese*)

Husband and wife are one flesh.
(*Yiddish*)

Even a melon seed may come between
husband and wife.
(*Iranian*)

If a woman is cold, it is her
husband's fault.
(*Russian*)

The wife is the keeper of her
husband's soul.
(*Egyptian*)

A man's best fortune, or his worst,
is his wife.
(*English*)

A good husband may have a bad wife,
and a bad husband may have a good wife.
(*Indian—Tamil*)

A young maid married to an old man
is like a new house thatched
with old straw.
(*English*)

49

A woman without a man is like a fish
without a bicycle.
(*American*)

A tent without a wife is like a
fiddle without a string.
(*Rumanian*)

A bad wife is the shipwreck
of her husband.
(*German*)

Leave her now and then if you would
really love your wife.
(*Malaysian*)

A woman without a husband is like a
distaff without the spindle.
(*Rumanian*)

The husband must not see, and the
wife must be blind.
(*English*)

A man without a wife is a man
without thoughts.
(*Finnish*)

Husbands are in heaven whose
wives chide not.
(*English*)

A woman without a mate is like
a garden without enclosure.
(*Slovakian*)

A good Jill may mend the bad Jack.
(*English*)

The conversation between husband
and wife no one knows about.
(*African—Ashanti*)

A good wife makes a good husband.
(*English*)

A man without a wife is but
half a man.
(*English*)

If you're faithful to your wife,
you'll have a healthy body.
(*Yiddish*)

The righteous woman has
only one husband.
(*Vietnamese*)

Maids want nothing but husbands.
(*English*)

Every Jack has his Jill.
(*English*)

There's one fool at least in
every married couple.
(*English*)

Happy the marriage where the husband
is the head and the wife the heart.
(*Estonian*)

He who does not honor his wife
dishonors himself.
(*Spanish*)

In bed, husband and wife;
out of bed, guests.
(*Chinese*)

The calmest husbands make
the stormiest wives.
(*English*)

A woman without a husband is like
a boat without a helmsman.
(*Vietnamese*)

Better be an old man's darling than
become a young man's slave.
(*English*)

If the wife sins, the husband
is not innocent.
(*Italian*)

LOVE AND KISSES

Frequent kisses end in a baby.
(*Hungarian*)

Stolen kisses are sweetest.
(*English*)

No woman is so old that she is not
pleased when she is kissed.
(*Slovakian*)

Nobody can refuse an honorable kiss.
(*German*)

A cunning person's kiss is like
that of a mosquito.
(*Rumanian*)

Kisses are like almonds.
(*Maltese*)

Nobody wants to kiss when
they are hungry.
(*English*)

He who has no money can neither
embrace nor kiss.
(*Moroccan*)

A kiss must last long to be enjoyed.
(*Greek*)

Kissing goes by favor.
(*English*)

Memory does not forget the promised
kiss, but the remembrance of the
kiss received is soon lost.
(*Finnish*)

She that will kiss will do worse.
(*English*)

A legal kiss is never as good as
a stolen one.
(*French*)

Kisses are the messengers of love.
(*Danish*)

Many kiss the child for the nurse's sake.
(*English*)

Love's mouth also kisses the dog.
(*German*)

Where cobwebs are plenty,
kisses are scarce.
(*English*)

A kiss is nothing when the
heart is mute.
(*French*)

After kissing comes more kindness.
(*English*)

A woman kissed is half married.
(*French*)

Not every kiss comes from the heart.
(*German*)

Kisses are keys.
(*English*)

To caress is the same as to kiss.
(*Russian*)

Kisses are first, and cusses come later.
(*Mexican*)

He that kisses his wife in the
marketplace will have many teachers.
(*English*)

Never kiss the maid if you can
kiss the mistress.
(*English*)

Embraces and kisses don't make
children, but they are the forerunners.
(*Spanish*)

For the sake of the knight the lady
kisses the squire.
(*French*)

A kiss of the mouth often touches
not the heart.
(*English*)

To eat without salt is to kiss one
you don't love.
(*Russian*)

Love starts with kisses and
ends with scars.
(*German*)

You don't know a woman without
having kissed her.
(*Russian*)

56

A man may kiss his cow.
(*English*)

Wanton kisses are the keys to sin.
(*English*)

A kiss of the lips doesn't always
come from the heart.
(*French*)

A forced kiss is like a corn
on the foot.
(*German*)

Kissing a married man is not sweet.
(*Russian*)

Do not make me kiss, and you will
not make me sin.
(*English*)

HATE AND JEALOUSY

Mistrust is an axe at the tree of love.
(*Russian*)

Love's merchandise is jealousy
and broken faith.
(*Italian*)

Love expels jealousy.
(*French*)

No hate is ever as strong as that
which stems from love.
(*German*)

Jealousy starts from the eye.
(*African—Zulu*)

Love as though you might have to
hate; hate as though you might
have to love.
(*Greek*)

No rose without a thorn, nor love
without a rival.
(*Turkish*)

The jealousy of a wife is the key
to her divorce.
(*Egyptian*)

Hatred is blind as well as love.
(*English*)

Jealousy is the life of love.
(*Japanese*)

Hot love is seldom without jealousy.
(*Italian*)

Love is full of busy fear.
(*English*)

He who cannot hate cannot love.
(*German*)

Love beyond measure afterward
brings hatred.
(*Rumanian*)

59

Loving one who loves another is
a bellyful of trouble.
(*African—Hausa*)

There was never great love that was
not followed by great hate.
(*Irish*)

A lewd bachelor makes
a jealous husband.
(*English*)

Love's anger is fuel to love.
(*German*)

It is better to have a husband
without love than to be jealous.
(*Italian*)

Love and show, hate and hide.
(*Egyptian*)

Three things breed jealousy: a mighty
state, a rich treasure, and a fair wife.
(*American*)

Hot love, hasty vengeance.
(*English*)

Jealousy is the sister of love.
(*French*)

A woman who has lost her rival
has no sorrow.
(*African—Wolof*)

The greatest hate springs from
the greatest love.
(*English*)

A lover's anger is short-lived.
(*Italian*)

In the eyes of the jealous,
a mushroom grows into a palm tree.
(*Russian*)

The more violent the love, the more
violent the anger.
(*Burmese*)

Where there's no jealousy,
there's no love.
(*German*)

Anger increases love.
(*Italian*)

Love is never without jealousy.
(*Scottish*)

A loving man, a jealous man.
(*Italian*)

Love yourself, others will hate you;
hate yourself, others will love you.
(*African—Hausa*)

Love conceals ugliness, and hate
sees a lot of faults.
(*Irish*)

Love lives a short while, but hate
lives for long.
(*Irish*)

When distrust enters in at the foregate,
love goes out at the postern.
(*English*)

A white mare needs washing;
a pretty wife, watching.
(*Latvian*)

THE FOOD OF LOVE

Love is meat and drink, and a
blanket to boot.
(*American*)

One cannot live on love
and fresh water.
(*French*)

A blow from our lover is as sweet
as the eating of raisins.
(*Egyptian*)

Lips however rosy must be fed.
(*English*)

One cannot live by love alone.
(*Polish*)

With a bottle and a girl, one does
not count the hours.
(*Polish*)

Lovers live by love as larks
live by leeks.
(*English*)

Love is full of honey and gall.
(*Slovenian*)

Love is sweet, but it's nice to
have bread with it.
(*Yiddish*)

Good wine and a pretty wife are two
sweet poisons to a man.
(*Rumanian*)

Love is the salt of life.
(*Philippine*)

Love and brandy have soothing
aftereffects both.
(*Mexican*)

Love does not fill the stomach.
(*Czech*)

No herb will cure love.
(*English*)

The love of a woman, and a bottle
of wine, are sweet for a season,
but last for a time.
(*English*)

Love is like butter, it's
good with bread.
(*Yiddish*)

Too much love and too much honey
spoil the stomach.
(*German*)

Honey on the tongue, gall
in the heart.
(*Yiddish*)

Love passes, hunger comes.
(*French*)

Of soup and love the first
is the best.
(*English*)

Love and eggs should be fresh
to be enjoyed.
(*Russian*)

He who has not tasted bitter,
knows not what sweet is.
(*German*)

The way to a man's heart is
through his stomach.
(*English*)

Without bread and salt, love
cannot exist.
(*Polish*)

A lovelorn cook oversalts the porridge.
(*German*)

Dry bread is better with love than
a fat capon with fear.
(*English*)

Love and hunger don't dwell together.
(*Yiddish*)

Without bread and wine even
love will pine.
(*French*)

HEARTACHES

Curse not your wife in the evening,
or you will have to sleep alone.
(*Chinese*)

Forced love does not last.
(*Dutch*)

Faults are thick where love is thin.
(*English*)

When misfortune comes in at the
door, love flies out of the window.
(*German*)

Love and foolishness differ from
each other only in name.
(*Hungarian*)

Every heart has its own ache.
(*English*)

Absence is a foe to love.
(*Italian*)

To love and to be wise are two
different things.
(*French*)

It is easy to reconcile when
there is love.
(*Welsh*)

All is fair in love and war.
(*English*)

New loves drive out the old.
(*Spanish*)

Though they rest on the same bed,
they dream of different things.
(*Korean*)

The lover who suffers not anguish
knows not the worth of pleasure.
(*Turkish*)

Love makes time pass away, and time
makes love pass away.
(*French*)

Little love, little trust.
(*English*)

A lovers' quarrel is short-lived.
(*Greek*)

The married man has many cares,
the unmarried one many more.
(*Finnish*)

Love suffers many disappointments.
(*Maltese*)

Lovers seek willingly new roads;
the married seek the old.
(*Russian*)

True lovers are shy when
people are by.
(*English*)

The only victory over love is flight.
(*French*)

Smoke and a scolding woman drive
a man out of the house.
(*Rumanian*)

By day they're ready to divorce,
by night they're ready to bed.
(*Yiddish*)

69

Out of sight, out of mind.
(*English*)

Lovers' quarrels are love redoubled.
(*Portuguese*)

Love is a dark pit.
(*Hungarian*)

The course of true love never
did run smooth.
(*English*)

The quarrels of married couples and
the west wind stop at evening.
(*Japanese*)

In love, as in war, each man must
gain his own victories.
(*American*)

Follow love and it will flee; flee
love and it will follow thee.
(*English*)

Love does not choose the blade of
grass on which it falls.
(*African—Zulu*)

Be off with the old love before
you are on with the new.
(*English*)

The remedy for love is—land between.
(*Spanish*)

No love without pain.
(*German*)

War, hunting, and love are as full
of troubles as pleasures.
(*English*)

Where there is love, there is
also a quarrel.
(*Rumanian*)

He who forces love where none
is found remains a fool the
whole year 'round.
(*German*)

One love expels another.
(*English*)

No thief steals love, but love
often makes thieves.
(*Swedish*)

A fence between makes love more keen.
(*German*)

There is no narrow road for the man
who truly loves.
(*Philippine*)

Three things drive a man out of
his house: smoke, rain, and
a scolding wife.
(*English*)

Every couple is not a pair.
(*English*)

There are no trials till marriage.
(*Irish*)

Love without return is like a
question without an answer.
(*German*)

Unlucky in love, lucky at play.
(*English*)

It is all one whether you die of
sickness or of love.
(*Italian*)

Love is shown by deeds, not by words.
(*Philippine*)

Love is a sweet torment.
(*English*)

If love is a sickness, patience
is the remedy.
(*African—Fulani*)

72

LOVE AND MONEY

Money without love is like salt
without pilchers.
(*English*)

Copper money makes rusty love.
(*Russian*)

Who wives for a dowry resigns
his own power.
(*French*)

Love lasts as long as the money endures.
(*English*)

When poverty crosses the threshold,
love flies out of the window.
(*African—Swahili*)

Money gets the bride.
(*Lebanese*)

He that is needy when he is married
shall be rich when he is buried.
(*English*)

Love can do much, money can do all.
(*German*)

No money, no mistress.
(*English*)

A poor man who marries a wealthy
woman gets a ruler and not a wife.
(*Greek*)

First thrive and then wive.
(*English*)

A thatched cottage with love is
still better than a tile-roofed
castle without it.
(*Vietnamese*)

Money is the sinew of love as
well as of war.
(*English*)

Love, grief, and money cannot
be kept secret.
(*Spanish*)

Who marries for love without money
has merry nights and sorry days.
(*English*)

Money, wine, and women bring about
the destruction of man.
(*Philippine*)

A poor beauty finds more lovers
than husbands.
(*English*)

It doesn't cost anything to promise
and to love.
(*Yiddish*)

Money makes marriage.
(*English*)

A rich man is never ugly in the
eyes of a girl.
(*French*)

Poverty and love are hard to conceal.
(*Norwegian*)

Love is not found in the market.
(*English*)

Love does wonders, but money
makes a marriage.
(*French*)

He that marries for wealth
sells his liberty.
(*English*)

When poverty enters from the window,
love goes out the door.
(*Maltese*)

Great wealth will marry off even
an old woman.
(*Yiddish*)

He who marries a woman for her
money is good for nothing.
(*Lebanese*)

A poor wedding is a prologue to misery.
(*English*)

He that marries for money, earns it.
(*English*)

Money separates love.
(*German*)

Labor is light where love does pay.
(*English*)

He who has not married nor built
a house doesn't know where his
money has gone.
(*Libyan*)

THE EYES OF LOVE

To the partial eyes of a lover,
pockmarks seem like dimples.
(*Japanese*)

It is only the blind who ask why
they are loved who are fair.
(*Danish*)

Good looks of a woman are her dowry.
(*Maltese*)

Love blinds itself to all shortcomings.
(*Lebanese*)

If Jack's in love, he's no judge
of Jill's beauty.
(*English*)

77

Loving comes by looking.
(*English*)

You can tell lovers from their faces.
(*African—Ovambo*)

A maiden should pretty herself for
a strange bachelor and a young
wife for her own husband.
(*Yiddish*)

Love is no impartial judge.
(*Irish*)

Love enters man through his eyes;
woman through her ears.
(*Polish*)

Sometimes love has been implanted
by one glance alone.
(*Egyptian*)

A woman is attractive when she is
somebody else's wife.
(*African—Shona*)

Love is blind.
(*English*)

A fair bride needs little finery.
(*Norwegian*)

78

Beauty does not ensnare men;
they ensnare themselves.
(*Chinese*)

She that is born a beauty
is half married.
(*English*)

Love overlooks defects, and hatred
magnifies shortcomings.
(*Lebanese*)

Love is blind to blemishes and faults.
(*Irish*)

Looks breed love.
(*English*)

Lovers think that others have no eyes.
(*Spanish*)

Whomever we love is clean even
when unwashed.
(*Russian*)

Beauty is in the eye of the beholder.
(*English*)

The man without eyes is no
judge of beauty.
(*Irish*)

Where there's no love, all
faults are seen.
(*German*)

That which is loved is always beautiful.
(*Norwegian*)

A lover is unmindful of any
charcoal on the body.
(*African—Annang*)

A pretty face doesn't make for
a good wife.
(*Yiddish*)

He who loves you won't
see your faults.
(*African—Hausa*)

She who loves an ugly man thinks
him handsome.
(*Spanish*)

Love starts from the eyes.
(*Russian*)

Love sees no faults.
(*English*)

Nobody's sweetheart is ugly.
(*Dutch*)